WA

Level 1
Early Beginner

CLOUDY
with a chance of
MEAT BALLS

Popcorn
ELT
Readers

Meet ...
everyone from

CLOUDY
with a chance of
MEAT BALLS

Flint

Flint Lockwood lives in Swallow Falls. He loves to invent.

Flint's dad

Sam

Sam Sparks is a weather girl on TV.

Steve

Flint has one friend. His name is Steve.

The mayor of Swallow Falls

The mayor wants tourists to come to Swallow Falls.

hot dog

meatball

spaghetti

burger

sardines

ice cream

sardine factory

There is a sardine factory in Swallow Falls. The people eat a lot of sardines.

Oh no! Sardines again!

Before you read ...
What do you think? What does Flint Lockwood invent?

New Words

What do these new words mean? Ask your teacher or use your dictionary.

food

There is a lot of **food**.

cloud / cloudy

It's **cloudy**!

There are a lot of **clouds**.

invent / invention

He loves to **invent**. This is his new **invention**.

fly

They can **fly**.

people

There are four **people**.

snow

It's **snowing!**

tourist

A lot of **tourists** come here.

spray-on

He has **spray-on** blue hair.

weather

The **weather** is good!

storm

It is a bad **storm**.

'What's for dinner?'

What's for **dinner**?

CHAPTER ONE
The Food Machine

Swallow Falls is a very quiet town. It is cloudy and it rains a lot there.

'We want tourists!' says the mayor. 'Come and see the sardine factory!'

But no tourists come.

Flint Lockwood loves to invent.

He invents a new car.
He wants to fly in it.

He invents new shoes.
They are spray-on shoes.

But there is always a problem with Flint's inventions. His car does not fly. His spray-on shoes never come off.

The people of Swallow Falls laugh at Flint.

Now Flint has a new invention. It is the Food Machine.

'Look!' says Flint to his dad. 'Water goes in here. And food comes out!'

'Oh no!' says Flint's dad.

'I can make food for everyone,' says Flint. 'No more sardines!'

'Burger, please!' Flint says to the Food Machine.

CRASH! BANG! BOOM!

'Oh no!' shouts Flint.

The Food Machine flies into the clouds.

'No more inventions!' says Flint's dad. 'Please!'

CHAPTER TWO
Food weather

It is cloudy in Swallow Falls. Then it starts to rain. It rains burgers!

'It's the Food Machine!' shouts Flint. 'The water from the clouds goes in. And food comes out!'

Sam Sparks comes to Swallow Falls.

'Look at this, everyone!' she says. 'It's raining burgers!'

'Your food weather is cool!' she says to Flint. 'Can you do breakfast?'

'Of course,' says Flint.

Flint goes to his computer.

'Breakfast, please!' he says to the Food Machine in the clouds.

In the morning, it rains breakfast!

'Come and have breakfast at Swallow Falls!' says Sam on the TV.

The people of Swallow Falls are happy.
One day it snows ice cream.
'Thank you, Flint!' the people say.

The mayor loves the food weather. He eats a lot.

'We want tourists in Swallow Falls!' says the mayor. 'They can come and see the food weather! What's for dinner, Flint?'

A lot of tourists come. 'We love Swallow Falls!' they say. 'And we love Flint Lockwood!'

But Flint's dad is not happy. 'The people are eating a lot of food,' he says. 'It's not good. Stop the Food Machine!'

'No!' says Flint. 'The people love it!'

CHAPTER THREE
The spaghetti storm

One day it rains hot dogs.

'These hot dogs are very big,' says Flint's dad.

'Oh no!' says Flint.

Flint goes to his computer. The mayor is there.

'Big is good,' says the mayor. 'I love big food.'

'No!' shouts Flint. 'It's not good.'

But there is a problem with the computer.

'I can't stop it!' says Flint.

It is very windy in Swallow Falls. A storm is starting.

'It's a spaghetti storm,' says Sam. 'And it's going to New York … and to London … and to China!'

'I can fly up to the Food Machine!' says Flint, and he starts to invent.

Soon he has a new flying car.

'I'm coming too!' says Sam.

Flint and Sam fly into the clouds!

The clouds are red and blue.
'Look!' says Flint. 'A big meatball!'
'Fly into it!' shouts Sam.

'It's very hot in here!' says Sam. 'Look! Is that the Food Machine?'

'Yes!' says Flint.

'How can you stop it?' asks Sam.

'That's no problem!' says Flint. 'I can stop it with my spray-on shoes. They never come off!'

The storm stops and the sun comes out in Swallow Falls.

'Yes!' shouts Flint's dad.

Sam and Flint fly home.

Everyone is happy.

'You're home!' says Flint's dad.

'Thank you, Flint!' the people say .

THE END

SUNNY DAYS AND RAINY DAYS

Sam Sparks is a weather girl. She likes sunny days, rainy days and food weather! How about you?

rain

This plant drinks a lot of water. It likes the rain! Do you like the rain?

shadow

sun

Do you like the sun? Go outside and look at your shadow. Is your shadow behind you or in front of you? Where is the sun?

clouds

Look at the clouds and find out about the weather. Do you see these clouds on a sunny or rainy day?

Look outside! Is it a rainy day or a windy day? Can you draw it?

wind

Do you like to go outside on a windy day? Of course! But sometimes wind is dangerous. This is a tornado. There are 1,000 tornadoes in the USA in a year.

tornado

snowflake

snow

Do you like the snow? Look at these snowflakes. All snowflakes have six sides.

What do these words mean? Find out.
outside   plant   rainbow   dangerous   side

After you read

1 Complete the sentences.

a) Flint Lockwood   i) eats a lot.

b) Sam Sparks   ii) loves to invent.

c) The Mayor   iii) eat a lot of sardines.

d) Flint's dad   iv) is a weather girl.

e) The people of Swallow Falls   v) doesn't like food weather.

2 True (✓) or False (✗)? Write in the box.

a) Sam Sparks is on TV. ✓

b) The mayor doesn't like the food weather.

c) A lot of tourists come to Swallow Falls.

d) The tourists love eating sardines.

e) There is an ice cream storm.

f) Flint invents a new flying car.

g) Flint's dad flies into the clouds.

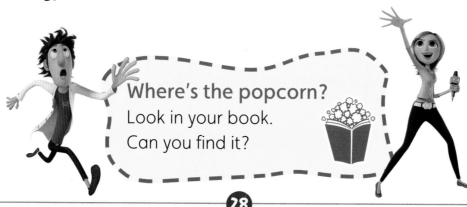

Where's the popcorn?
Look in your book.
Can you find it?

Puzzle time!

1 What food can you see in the rain?

burger   hot dog   ice cream   ~~sardine~~   spaghetti

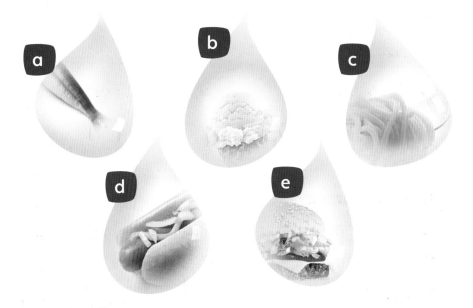

a) sardine   b) ....   c) ....

d) ....   e) ....

2a What food do you like? Circle the words.

i) I *love* / *like* / *don't like* burgers.

ii) I *love* / *like* / *don't like* ice cream.

iii) I *love* / *like* / *don't like* sardines.

b Now complete the sentence.

My favourite food is ....

3a What is the weather? Complete the words.

a

It's **s** _ _ _ **y**.

b

It's a **s** _ _ _ **m**.

c

It's **c** _ _ _ **d y**. [1]

d

It's **s** _ _ _ _ _ **g**.

b What comes first in the story? Put the weather in order.

4 How does the Food Machine work? Read the sentences and draw pictures.

Water from the clouds goes in.

Food comes out.

Imagine...

Imagine you have a Food Machine. Put water in the machine. What food comes out? Mime it! Can your friends guess the food?

breakfast   a burger   a hot dog   ice cream
a meatball   a sardine   spaghetti

Chant

1 🅣7 **Listen and read.**

What's for dinner?

Monday, Tuesday,
It's a cloudy day.
What's for dinner?
Meatballs!

Wednesday, Thursday,
It's a rainy day.
What's for dinner?
Burgers!

Friday, Saturday,
It's a snowy day.
What's for dinner?
Ice cream!

Sunday, oh no!
It's a stormy day.
What's for dinner?
Spaghetti!

2 🅣8 **Say the chant.**